This novel is a work of fiction. All the
characters, organizations, establishments, and
events portrayed in this novel are either product
of the author's imagination or are fiction.

Copyright © 2013 by Michelle Murray

Published by:
GOOD2GO PUBLISHING
7311 W. Glass Lane
Laveen, AZ 85339
www.good2gopublishing.com
twitter @good2gobooks
G2G@good2gopublishing.com
Facebook.com/good2gopublishing
ThirdLane Marketing: Brian James
Brian@good2gopublishing.com

ISBN: 978-0-9891859-3-6

All Scriptures, quotations are taken from the King James
Version of the Bible.

Healing

In The Midst Of Adversity

Michelle Murray

DEDICATION

This book is dedicated to all those that are having a wilderness experience, and going through the fiery trials of life. Take courage, God's Grace is sufficient for you.

"His power is made perfect in weakness"
2 Corinthians 12.9

But they that wait upon the Lord shall renew their strength; they shall mount up with wings as eagles; thy shall run, and not be weary; and they shall walk and not faint. (Isaiah 40:31)

Table of Contents

Introduction: To the Reader
Thank You
About the Author

Salvation
A gift from God

Songs of Deliverance

Thank You
Introduction: To The Reader

Writing is a gift and a talent that God has given to me. God is pleased when we use our talents to enhance the Kingdom of God. So many stumbling blocks and obstacles I have had to face, and through His Word God has taught me how to endure in the midst of trials and tribulations. Going through this process, God has healed me in many areas because I had to submit more to God and resist the devil.

In the course of studying the Word of God, I began to learn Godly principles that work which are necessary to winning:
• Taking care of my family
• Having peace and joy at times that I should be sad and full of stress
• Building faith in Jesus more every day.

My desire is that every reader will receive strength, knowledge and understanding of God's Word, and be more of an overcomer by my testimony and know that God is no respecter of persons and that what He does for one He will do for someone else.

Romans 8:35-37 says: 'Who shall separate us from the love of Christ? shall tribulation, or distress, or persecution, or famine, or nakedness, or peril, or sword? As it is written, For thy sake we are killed all the day long we are accounted as sheep for the slaughter. My, in all these things we are more than conquerors through him that loved us."

I give thanks and praise to my Lord, Jesus Christ who has given me the ability to see my dreams come to pass. Huge thanks to my children William Buckhana, Mitchell Murray, Marcus Murray, and Trachelle Murray for their love and patience, as we endured so many fiery trials.

Also, I thank my Pastor, Darrell D. Elligan, of the True Light Baptist Church who has poured much spiritual wisdom and knowledge into my life. I thank all of the True Light family, a church where miracles really do happen.

Furthermore, special thanks to all my brothers and sisters from the Ames house of prayer. I would like to give a special recognition and thanks to composer Stanton Lather for providing the peaceful melodies of Abiding and Beloved from his CD "Walking In The Light."

Big thanks to Jackey Washington, who worked diligently and faithfully in supporting me. Much thanks to Missionary Constance Watson for her Missionary Training and Outreach.

Chapter One

Amazing Grace Testimony

Amazing Grace is my testimony declaring there is nothing too hard for God. No matter what your situation is or what circumstances you are facing, what matters is that God can save you from the gutter most to the uttermost. God is never late, but on time.

His grace is sufficient for you. (Hebrews 7:25).

My life was not too different from most people's lives. It was filled with many disappointments and daily struggles of trying to live in a dysfunctional family in New York City, Harlem area, where drug use and selling was very common.

I suffered much lack and I never really had any money, As I attended school, I was blessed to have teachers that believed in me. They have always inspired me to stay in school, and seek after the American dream. So I bought into it. I went to work part-time and continued going to school.

In 1983, I graduated college and received an Associate's degree. I started a good paying job working as a secretary at McGraw-Hill, Inc. At that time, my family had been evicted and had to move in with my aunt in the projects. Living with my aunt were her 2 daughters, and their 3 children along with my mother, my sister and her 2 children, and 7 cats.

After graduating, this was the moment that I had been waiting all my life. I had been working and enduring for the opportunity to leave home and receive the American dream, to put my past behind me, and float on. I welcomed this opportunity with open arms.

I had achieved much and I had everything I was taught you needed to live the American dream. I had a college degree, a good paying job, good credit, saving and checking accounts, clean criminal record. I was drug and alcohol free, full of life, energy, and had great expectations.

As I stepped out to gain all that I had worked so hard to achieve, I found myself faced with many disappointments, which began to take my life in another direction.

I went to get an apartment, but because I lived in NY, most apartments in downtown Manhattan were very small and expensive. The apartments in Harlem were very dangerous to live in alone. You had drug dealers on the corner, rats and roaches in most apartments, and unfriendly neighbors. I tried to move into the projects, and all the decent apartments go by a waiting list that's usually a 5-year waiting list. In addition, you had to have at least one child to even qualify.

This really frustrated me and I began to try to get out another way. I began to date men that had their own apartments - men that looked like they had it going on.

After a period of time, this just led me to having four children out of wedlock and having to get public assistance for food, WIC and Medicaid.
I continued to keep a job, yet was faced with the difficulty of paying for childcare and struggling as a single parent. Most of my dreams had been shattered. I was home bound very distressed from the cares of life, and taking care of 4 children.

After being on the waiting list for so many years, I made it into the projects. I spent a lot of my money on the cost of living. I was frustrated at some of the bad choices I had made which led me to a very depressed state of mind.

Although I was a young good looking mother, I still enjoyed life. After growing up with a family that partied all the time, I began to want to experience what that life was like since everything else had disappointed me. This couldn't possibly hurt. I believed I was strong and capable, you know, and deserved to have a good time like everyone else. Why should I be the only one working hard? I paid my dues, and I deserved to have a little fun is what I told myself.

I began to go to house parties in the projects, visit different neighbor's houses and stay out late at night. I lost interest in working because I was enjoying the nightlife. It was not long before I began to experiment with the drug called cocaine.

Very popular with the men. Cocaine relieved me from many of my failures, heartaches, and problems.

As time passed, I began to indulge heavily in cocaine and was becoming everything I did not want to be; broke, a hustler, a liar, misfit mother, and very promiscuous. As I realized the state of my condition I decided to make a choice to rehabilitate myself.

The first thing I tried was to turn to a man who seemed to love me, and all of my children. He kept a job, and didn't get as high as I did. I thought that would help me to gain strength and make a change. This became one of the biggest mistakes in my life.

This man began to abuse me mentally, often using all types of profanity to talk to me, constantly disrespecting me in front o of my children and other people, ridiculing me for all of my failures. When I tried to put him out he would put crazy glue in my locks so I couldn't lock my doors, throw bottles down my hall making loud and outrageous noises, and writing obscene words with a marker on my front door. This type of humiliation and abuse led me to getting even higher and out of control. At this point, it just didn't seem like I was going to ever succeed so I signed myself into a rehabilitation center called Odyssey House for Women and Children. I spent 3 weeks of thinking about my life and I wanted to try again. So I signed myself out, and returned home to my 2 bedroom apartment in the projects.

My condition did not get any better, and I often thought of leaving the state of New York. I wanted to relocate for the first time- kind of like a bird wanting to fly away. My sister, who just would up and leave, landed in the state of Georgia.

She called me and invited me to come to Atlanta, Georgia. I thought that was just what I needed, and I took a plane the next month. I arrived in the state of Georgia on March 1, 1994. This was the turning point of my life.

I loved Georgia, and I made up my mind the first day that I was here to stay. I stayed away from drugs for about two months. I got a job at McDonald's and a two-bedroom townhouse. In the month of June, my children were able to join me.

At first, everything was going well in Georgia. I began to meet new friends. But once again I began to compromise and indulge heavily in using cocaine. I lost my job, DFCS (the Department of Family and Children's Services) took 2 of my younger children, and I was evicted from my home. All my dreams had been shattered. I had no choice but to live in a shelter.

My behavior had not changed, and I continued to get high. I was constantly evicted from my apartments every

3 months, and with 4 children, I lived in 5 different shelters throughout Atlanta. Many of the churches would help support me with food, and I would sometimes sit in on their Bible study. There was one particular message that always stood out, which was that Jesus came that I might have life, and have it more abundantly.

After I moved into my new apartment, I began to remember the message that I had heard. I thought about cleaning up my life. I went back to work, and when I received my next paycheck, I thought I would just reward myself with just a little drink. Before the night was over, I had spent all my money and I was at the worst point in my life. I was tired and had enough. I was full of despair, and very much ashamed of myself. I felt like I just didn't want to live anymore. Suddenly, I began to remember the message, Jesus saying "I came to give you life," and I began to cry out to the Lord, "What life is this that You came to give me, because my life is a mess and if there is a better life I want it!"

Shortly after, I was evicted once again, and I sent my children back to New York to live because all my hopes and dreams were gone. I was tired, and I just didn't know what to do, but go to another shelter.

I was accepted into the Salvation Army shelter, and that's when I began to think more about the life Jesus came to give me. I began to search for this life and I went to Bible study at the shelter. I went to all kinds of different church services, breakthrough conferences, and listened to spiritual wisdom and encouragement from people who professed to know Christ. I still did not receive this life. My situation began to take a turn for the worse. I lost my job and was not able to get an apartment because of so many evictions. I was not eligible for much assistance because I did not have my kids with me.

I was alone, angry, disappointed and full of much despair. That's when suicide became very real to me. My life had totally fallen apart, and I just did not see the point or reason to continue to live. There was no one or any way I could repair it.

I received my last paycheck and set out to go in the area of East Point (a suburb of Atlanta). I was going to hang out one last time and just allow myself to overdose, and get it over with.

On the way to East Point, I saw a church that had a large sign up and it said "Holy Convocation." I had never heard of that before, so I said that maybe I would go inside, "because you just never know"

The speaker was Bishop Clarence McClendon, and he prophesied: "That the sickness you have is not unto death, but for the glory of God." He said to "Believe, because that which you ask God for, He is going to do."

That night I went back to the shelter because I had never heard that voice before that seemed so real.

The next day, which was Saturday morning, I was expecting God to show up, but nothing happened. Just when I was about to give up on God and everything else, a very nice couple approached me and invited me to go to church. Because I felt that I did not have a life and was on my way to committing suicide, I thought I would delay the process. I went with the couple. As we were in the church, which was a gym, the woman began to say, "God is going to deliver someone from cocaine."

I began to look around at the others because I just couldn't believe she was talking about me. In my mind my life was over; so good for someone else. I never answered the call and they continued with the service. After a while, they began to call people up to the front to deliver them from their habits like drinking and smoking. I went up to the front along with the others, and a man came to me and said, "You are that cocaine addict God wants to deliver."

Right away I panicked and began to suggest he not tell everyone in the church. Immediately he called a man over to me, and the man smiled and said, "You are about to be blessed." He said, "Lift your hands," and he placed one hand on my head and another on my stomach. He prayed for me, and instantaneously I was delivered from cocaine, and filled with the Holy Ghost.

I felt the power of the living God enter into me, and I began to break down and cry. I heard the voice of Jesus say, "You do not have to worry about your past. You are with me now. Enter into the light, and receive the life that I came to give you, an abundant life."

When I left the church that afternoon which was held at a neighborhood gym, everything seemed different. The sky was brighter, the grass was greener, the birds were singing, and I felt loved. I knew without a doubt that I had received the life Jesus came to give me because I now had the presence of God living on the inside of me in the form of the Holy Spirit which gives life. I was now in the process of being restored back to the place God had originally meant for me to be.

Shortly after, I received a 3-bedroom apartment. I had all my kids returned back to me. I received a job in Buckhead and I became a member of a church called The True Light Baptist Church where miracles really do happen.

I know for sure that there is nothing impossible with God. He will never turn away a repentant heart. He is always standing by. When you call, He will always answer because He loves you. He came to give you life and life more abundantly. I can proudly say I have that life and it's full of love, peace, joy, goodness and mercy. God's Grace is truly Amazing.

Chapter Two

Seeking The King Before The Things

I was truly inspired to make known how important it is to seek first God's kingdom. God has so much in store for us. If we begin to desire those things that matter to God, and get to know His heart, we would seek to please God.

'There is no good thing that He will withhold from us that walk uprightly before Him." (Psalms 84:11).

So many times we overlook the Lord, and we do not really know how awesome, how great, and merciful is the Lord. He cares for His children like a father, and He has made every provision for you to live holy, righteous and have joy. The promise is in His Son, Jesus. He is the King of Kings and Lord of Lords. Repentance is what He called every one of us to do. to let go of our wicked and unrighteous ways, seek His face, and seek His way of living, which brings us into His peace that passes all understanding, and aligns us back into His will.

God is so good and wise, and He knows what's best for us even when we think we've got it all figured out. He steps in at the nick of time before we can destroy our lives, and truly mess up what God has planned for us. *Jeremiah 29:11 says,*

"For I know the thoughts that I think toward you, saith the LORD, thoughts of peace, and not of evil, to give you an expected end."

That Scripture provides hope because God tells you that He desires peace and there is an expected end to the hurt, pain, and sufferings that you have experienced. So we have to examine ourselves and our hearts to be obedient to His voice because God is on your side. He loves you and gave His son Jesus for you. He gave you a title deed called the Word of God (The Bible) which is God's will and plan for your life. What we need to do is seek the King, His kingdom and righteousness and all things shall be added to us because how can you lose anything if he owns it all. He is in control of all things. *Matthew 6:33)*

When we go through, it's uncomfortable because it takes us out of our comfort zones. God is stretching, molding, and preparing us for greatness. *(Psalms 71:21)* We think we need a lot of worldly possessions to live and be happy. These things are idols, and we put them before God, whether we know it or not. This is one of the reasons God will allow the enemy to attack you in certain areas so that we will seek God and pray, and believe Him for the things we need, and worship the Creator instead of the creation. *(Ecclesiastes 12:1)*

This also works a deeper faith inside of us where we move and live and have our being in Jesus Christ. *(Acts 17:28)* When we learn to live and do without the things we used to depend on, now God becomes our all-sufficient God, our El Shaddai, and now we begin to renew our minds and desire the things that please Him. God is now glorified because we now bear fruit that will last, and we begin to look a little more like Christ. *John 15:16)* God is concerned about everything that concerns you, but He will allow the adversary to destroy that which might be in the way of getting His will done. *(Psalms 138:8)*

Sometimes God will not change your situation, but He will change you in the midst of your situation. God has spoken too many of us, and sometimes, because of our rebellious ways and stubborn hearts, although we know that He has been telling us to do something or go somewhere we needed to go, we decide to do things our own way. God may have to knock you down so you can hear Him and do it His way. At that time, God knows He has your attention. The story of Jonah is a great example. *(Jonah1:17)*

Also, if you are under an attack, it is best to walk in alignment with God and change your strategy. Submit to God, and resist the devil. He will flee from you.
(James 4:7)

God is in absolute control, and He knows that character will be produced in and through you. God's purpose is to see you operating in the fruits of His spirit because you know the tree by the fruit it bears. *(Galatians 5:22-24)*

God blesses kingdom people. In order to possess the kingdom of God, it requires that you go through the process where three main aspects must come into agreement: your mind, body and soul.

Kingdom harvests start by tithing. Tithing brings you into covenant with God and God operates by His contract, which is the Bible.
When you sow your seed you can believe God for a miracle. Your harvest will return pressed down, shaken and running over shall men give into your bosom. You must
 know that the blessings of the Lord make you rich and add no sorrow. *(Proverbs 10:22)*

In order to receive life changing results, you have to seek the life changer. Jesus came to give you life and it more abut).-dandy. *John 10:10, 5:40)* Nothing you ever give to God goes wasted. It is always multiplied because God owns it all. Your faith brings you into receiving what God has, and obedience to God's word and tithing brings you into your harvest. *(Genesis 8:22, proverbs 3:9-10)*

When you get Jesus, you get all His promises and they are Yes and Amen. *(2 Corinthians 1:20)* When God asks you to do something and the flesh resists, and you don't want to do it, ask yourself these questions and make this comparison:

- Why am I resisting God?
- Do I believe and trust Him?
- What punishment can I afford for my disobedience?
- What blessing do I want to receive for my obedience?

Bring ye all the tithes into the storehouse ... and prove me ...
if I will not open you the windows of heaven, and pour you out a
blessing, that there shall not be room enough to receive it."
Malachi 3:10)

Deuteronomy 28:1-14 outlines the blessing and rewards for obedience. *Deuteronomy 28:15-68* outlines the cursing and punishments for disobedience. When your breakthrough comes, you will determine what you receive. For example, some of the children of Israel died in the wilderness because they did not believe and were disobedient to God. Those that were obedient to God entered into the promised land. Your future depends on the way you respond to the voice of God. God's voice is commonly heard through the five-fold ministry of Apostles, Prophets, Evangelists, Pastors, and Teachers. *(1 Corinthians 12:28, Ephesians 4:11)*

When you walk in God's alignment and in the order of God, you must be in the center of His Word, which is His will. When you are in an agreement and walking in obedience to God, the assignment given to you will always be greater than you. The majority will oppose because your situation will look like you will experience a disaster because the enemy is always trying to use fear to block your blessing. Faith is the remedy and antidote you need. *(Hebrews 11:6)* Always remember, you enter into the kingdom of God through much suffering because the flesh is always warring against the spirit. Doing it your way vs. doing it God's way.

God gave us the keys to the kingdom and instructions to win. So why are we being destroyed and living defeated lives? Maybe it's because you are hanging with people who have your problem because misery loves company. Start attaching yourself to people who have your answer.

We must work while it is day because we do not know when the night will come. *John* 9:4) We must also rest assured that our work is not in vain. God knows ALL and He sees ALL and His love endures forever. His mercies are new each and every day.

I know your heart may be broken and you may be torn apart because life seems so unfair. You always feel alone, burdened by the cares of this world. It seems like there is no way to get a break.

Jesus is the way, the truth, and the life, and you can lean on Him when you are not strong. He will be your friend. He will revive you, and comfort you and heal your wounds. *(Hosea 6:14)* He knows how much you can handle, and He knows your heart. He will not put more on you than you can bear. So feel free to turn to Jesus because He came to make you free. Receive the abundant life that He came to give you.

Know that you are   beloved, and He wants you to keep your joy because it won't be long before your change comes. It won't be long before you see the rain. It won't be long before every tear will be washed away.

Just stay encouraged and know that Jesus is a present help in the time of trouble. He is a strong tower where the righteous run to and are safe. He is a healer and wants you to die to your life that you may receive the greatest gift of all — His resurrected life on the inside of you. A new creation. The work of the Master.

So hold on and be strong because your help is on the way. Your breakthrough is today. Your faith has made you whole.

Prophecy,

I speak life into your situation. I say, Arise and go forth and fulfill the purpose God has planned for you. He has called you out of darkness and into His marvelous light. You don't need to be depressed because Jesus has come that you may have life and have it more abundantly. I speak life into your situation and say, Peace be still.

God is able to do exceedingly and abundantly above all you can think or ask and I command those dg bones to come alive, and your barren land to become fruitful this day. The devil is a liar. Your situation is not too hard for God. When it's too hard for you, you must know it's perfect for God. So stay encouraged. Jesus is never late and He is always on time, and this word was sent to you that you may lift up your head, 0 ye gates, and let the King of glory come in. Get yourself ready because you are about to receive a full manifestation of the Almighty coming to your rescue because

23

what you pray in secret, He will reward you openly. It doesn't matter the hour or the time. He is great, and He wishes above everything that you prosper, and be in good health just as your soul prospers.

What you are believing God for will come to pass. So get yourself ready because you no longer live in lack, and you no longer will be a reproach before men, you will no longer be intimidated by what Satan has used to try to demolish you, but you will live to declare the glory of God.

Be in expectancy because you are destined for greatness. No matter what it looks like or what it has been, I decree breakthrough in your finances, healing for your sorrows, wholeness in your body, restoration in your family and in your homes, loved ones restored. I command that you live in the land of plenty. All your substance shall be returned to you. I decree a prosperous future for you. You have a right to the tree of life. In Jesus' Name.

Chapter Three

The Violent Take It Back By Force

The violent take it back with the force of love,
peace, joy, kindness, patience and meekness.

`Let your light so shine blare men, that thy may see your good works, and glorify your Father which is in heaven." (Matthew 5:16)

Do you know what it would be like to dream your whole life away and never let a single dream come true? Well, let's start today because the dream is on the inside of you. Inside of us God has placed talents and gifts to be used to enhance other people's lives. *(1 Corinthians 7:7)*

The fulfillment you get is that you are living and being the person God has created you to be and that's enough to motivate a person that has no motivation. That's why every member is important to the Body of Christ. *(1Corinthinans 12:12-27)* Jesus the Christ who lives on the inside of you, the Spirit of truth, (1 *John 5:6)* the God of love, and the keeper of your soul. He is the God who keeps you in perfect peace *(Isaiah 26:3)* and gives you peace that passes all understanding *(Philippians 4:7)*

As you grow in His grace, you will see yourself blossoming and blooming in a way you never could before. You will not be afraid anymore of challenges, and you will be ready to see what's on the other side of that mountain. You will be ready to open up to love because I know without a doubt; you are more than a conqueror. You can live out your dreams because they are divine inspirations from God who created you in your mother's womb. *(Psalms 139:13)* He knew what you would be, how you would look, how you would think, and what mistakes you would make. God continues to instill the power on the inside of you to inspire you to live out every gift and every talent using the form of love because God is love, and He loves everybody. *(John 3:16)*

So as you enjoy your new life, and begin to break out of your shell, the world is not that strange because you have found your place. It is in the One who is the creator of all things, the Christ in you, the hope of glory which gives you the freedom to be you and to know that you are somebody special. *(Colossians 1:27)*

You are a child of the Most High and you can do all things through Jesus Christ who will give you the strength. *(Philippians 4:13)* You can walk with your head up because He has anointed you to live life victoriously and live it abundantly. You can raise your children because He has given you wisdom to be a parent and you have committed to being all that God has allowed you to be, free to live the life He planned for you. *Jeremiah 29:11)*

The Kingdom of God suffers violence, but the violent take it back by force! It's by grace that we are saved, not of ourselves that any man should boast. *(Ephesians 2:8-9)* There is none that is right, for we all have sinned and fallen short of God's glory. *(Romans 3:23)* But because God's grace is so sufficient, we receive a second change time and time again. When Jesus came into the world, He fulfilled and released us from the law *(Matthew 5:17, Romans 6:14)*. He brought truth and grace *(John 1:14)* and if He is the truth; then let every other spirit be a lie. *(John 14:17, 1 John 5:6)*

We all stand in need of God's grace and we ought not take His grace in vain *(2 Corinthians 6:1)* because the Kingdom of God is in you and God is making you, not you yourself. He has given us the victory and made us each an overcomer, because Jesus said,

"In the world ye shall have tribulation: but be of good cheer; I have overcome the world" (John 16:33)

This is letting you know you can do all things through Jesus Christ who will strengthen you. *(Philippians 4:13)* If you have been called to it, God will bring you through it. What is too hard for God? *(Genesis 18:14)*

So there is no need to fear because fear is only false evidence appearing to be real, and we must use faith to face our fears each and every day, because God has a plan and a purpose for your life. He is the way, the truth, and the life. *(John 14:6)* He has made you fearlessly beautiful *Palms 139:14)* and has given you the victory. So move forward, leave that which is behind, and press forward into the high calling to which you have been called. *(Philippians 3:14)* Your blessing is in the pressing.

You are God's creation, and it's His grace that will lead you all the way because He knows our weaknesses and all our insecurities, as well as our strengths. We have an advocate with the Father, who is a high priest and has known of all our infirmities. *(1 John 2:1)*

So put on the new man that's being transformed and renewed daily into the image of Christ. The Bible says *"that if any man is in Christ, he is a new creation. old things have passed away; all things are made new! "(2 Corinthians 5:17)*

This development takes place as we enter into the Kingdom of God through much suffering because the flesh is warring against the spirit. *Matthew 11:12)* That's why the kingdom suffered violence, but the violent take it back by force. The force is love, peace, gentleness, goodness, faith, meekness, self-control, joy and longsuffering, considered the fruits of the Spirit. *(Galatians 5:22-23)* Wherever there is fruit, there is life, and Jesus is the life so we need to examine our fruit and act extremely violent in walking in God's love, peace, and joy. If we do so, wherever we go we will impart life into dead situations. The Bible also says that you will know the tree by the fruit it bears. *(Matthew 12:33)*

The first step to taking back your life is admitting you have a problem. Get real with yourself and repent and turn your heart back to God. A broken and contrite spirit He will not turn away. *(Psalm 51:17)* Also, you have to believe that God can fix your problem. Earth has no sorrow Heaven can't heal. *(Psalms 103:34.)*

You have to truly believe that His love for you is unconditional, that while you were in your sin Jesus died for you because He loves you, and that He came to preach the good news that you have forgiveness of sin and to set the captives free. *(1 John 1:9)*

Praying to God is an awesome weapon needed to take back matters that are out of control in your life.

(Proverbs 15:8, 15:29) Praying is actually talking directly to God, and He said we have boldness to come boldly to the throne of grace, and whatever we pray, just ask and believe and you shall receive. (*Matthew 21:22*) So talk to God in prayer about everything because He already knows all things and He will guide you because He said that He will be a present help in the time of trouble.
(Psalms 46:1)

Faith is very necessary in receiving your answered prayer because God says that if you believe you shall receive.

Doubt and disbelief are two agents the devil will send to tear down your faith because he knows if you waver and are double-minded you don't need to expect to receive anything from God. *(James 1:6-8)* The way you please God is by believing in Him, and trusting in His word. *(Hebrews 11:6)* Faith comes by hearing and hearing by the word of God. *(Romans 10:17)* How can they hear unless they have a preacher?

(Romans 10:14) So it would be a good idea to ask God to lead you to a church where there is an anointed preacher that can pour wisdom, knowledge and understanding of God's word into your life and help you to grow spiritually. No Christian should be without a church home.

Praise is a weapon that will fight for you. God said,

> *"For everything that has breath to praise the Lord"(Psalms 150:6)*

Praise is preparing the right atmosphere in a spirit of excellence. When we praise God we prepare a place for Him to move on our behalf because God inhabits the praises of His people. *(Psalms 22:3)*

God enjoys watching His children rejoice over Him. *(Hebrews 13:15)* Praise and hell cannot stay in the same place. So when the devil is raising hell you must begin to raise a little heaven by praising God because when the praises go up you can guarantee the blessings will come down. Keep the high praise of "Hallelujah!" in your mouth. *(Psalms 149:6)*

God is the one fighting your battle. So take it back by force and know you have the victory!

Him to move on our behalf because God inhabits the praises of His people. *(Psalms 22:3)* God enjoys watching His children rejoice over Him. *(Hebrews 13:15)* Praise and hell cannot stay in the same place. So when the devil is raising hell you must begin to raise a little heaven by praising God because when the praises go up you can guarantee the blessings will come down. Keep the high praise of "Hallelujah!" in your mouth. *(Psalms 149:6)*

God is the one fighting your battle. So take it back by force and know you have the victory!

PROPHECY:

Be still as the waters calm you. It's a season of peace, longevity, and beauty. Everything that was worn out will be made new; everything lost will be restored. It's a season of a new you. You are His shepherd and you were made to prosper. You were equipped to be strong. You were born to succeed. Just as the deer pants for the brook, let your heart pant for the love of God. The Kingdom of God suffered violence, but the violent take it back by force. He has given you the power. Take authority.

Chapter Four

The Advocate vs. The Adversary

Too many times we focus on the adversary and our life circumstances. We let fear dominate and dictate the outcome.

We should be praising God that He has given us an advocate, Jesus, who is constantly interceding for us. *(1 John 2:1)*

So much spiritual warfare is going on and we Christians are losing sight of who we are and who's in charge. We are children of the living God. The Bible says,

> *Nat those who walk alter the spirit are the sons of God"*
> *(Romans 8:14)*

The Scriptures were written to help us grow spiritually, and come into the knowledge of the truth, and to apply the word of God to our lives, situations, and circumstances. *(2 Timothy *16, 17; Romans 15:4)*

The purpose of the word is to be used as a sword to cut down. *(Hebrews 4:12)* Also, the Bible said, "to *cast down every imagination that exalts itself against the truth and bring it into captivity and revenge it with the word of God"*

(2 Corinthians 10:4-5) So we as Christians have to get an understanding of the Bible, because the Bible gives instructions as to what we ought to do when trouble comes our way. *(Proverbs 23:12, Proverbs 4:13)*

Let's look at the definition of the adversary; He comes to steal, kill, and destroy. *(John 10:10)* He is a roaring lion seeking whom he may devour. *(1 Peter 5:8)* What is the devil's character? Satan is transformed as an angel of light. *(2 Corinthians 11:14)* The devil still has beauty, and wisdom, but it's corrupted. His name in heaven was Lucifer, which means bearer of light.

Just to give you a little history, God did not create a devil. God created an anointed cherub, a holy angel, appointed by God. *28:14-15)* Lucifer was full of beauty, music, and lights, and he was in charge of the heavenly choir. His beauty brought on pride and his heart was lifted up because of his beauty. Because iniquity entered into his heart, he was kicked out of heaven. *(Ezekiel 28:17)*

The devil's purpose is to abort the plan and destiny of the children of God. We are taught not to give him a foothold or any room in our lives. *(Ephesians 4:27)* The way we know that he is given a place or an entrance is we lose our joy. We become frustrated, angry, challenged, and bombarded on every side and we feel like we want to give up.

Satan is also the father of lies, and all he knows how to do is lie and deceive. *john 8:44)* Satan is the accuser of

33

the brethren. *(Revelation 12:10)* Satan wears a camouflage and his mission is to deceive the very elect. *(Matthew 24:24)* Satan is a counterfeit, and tries to imitate the Holy One. He is out to destroy the people of God and send as many people to hell because he knows his days are numbered.

A sure way to recognize the deceiver is he will not confess Jesus has come in the flesh. *(2 John 1:7)* The devil's intention is to manipulate the hearts and minds of people. He wants to cause them to fear because when you operate in fear you are not keeping the faith and without faith you cannot please God. *(Hebrews 11:6)* So the devil is constantly trying to <u>instill</u> fear in everything we do. Fear is false evidence appearing real. Also the devil's main agents are doubt and disbelief. If he can cause you to doubt God he has defeated you, so we must choose to walk in faith, and not fear. God has not given us a spirit of fear. He's given us love, power, and a sound mind.
(2 Timothy 1:7)

We must understand the reason for the spiritual battle that we are faced with daily. The flesh is constantly warring against the spirit. *(Romans 7:23)* The spirit has to have a body to live in and that's why we have to understand we do not actually wrestle against flesh and blood, but powers, principalities, and rulers in high places. *(Ephesians 6:12)* The word wrestling tells us you are going back and forth, tug-of-warring, and when we win each battle it increases our faith and enables us to have a deeper walk with the Lord. God is then glorified. The Bible tells us we go from faith to faith and glory to glory.

(Romans 1:17, 2 Corinthians 3:18) This is a true sign that we are growing and producing fruits of the spirit.

One of the fruits is longsuffering because it causes obedience. The Bible tells us that Jesus learned obedience by suffering and in the word obedience is the small word die. *(Hebrews 5:8)* So the pain you are actually experiencing is your flesh being crucified so that the Spirit

of the living God can rise up on the inside of you and produce life. *(John 6:63)*

Jesus is the Advocate, a high priest interceding for us. *(1 John 2:1)* Because Jesus was the word made flesh that walked amongst us *(John 1:14),* He is able to feel our infirmities. Jesus instructs us that in this world we will have trouble, but be of good cheer for He has overcome the world and has given you the victory. *john 16:33)* The name of Jesus is above all powers, principalities and rulers. (Philippians 2:9) He says to put on the whole armor of God so in the day of evil we can stand. *(Ephesians 6:11)*

The devil is defeated, but not destroyed. He has no power over you, only what power you give him. This happens when you doubt and disobey the word of God. The devil used this tactic to deceive Eve in the garden. *(Genesis 3:4-6)* Man lost dominion and was kicked out of the garden.

(Genesis 3:24) Jesus, who is called the second Adam, by shedding His blood on Calvary, reconciled mankind back unto God, which is salvation. *(Romans 5:10)* Jesus is the resurrection and the life. *(Phil 11:25)* Jesus is the Anointed One, and the anointing is the burden removing, yoke destroying, power of God. He gave us this power to destroy the devil.

(1 John 3:8)

We have to focus more on the Advocate, because if we want to go higher we are going to have to have a resurrected mind. As we focus on the Advocate, who is Jesus, we know that Jesus is the living word. So in order to produce change in our lives, we are going to have to activate the word because the Bible tells us that the word is alive and active and a two-edged *sword. (Hebre2vs 4:12)* This is actually the formula we need to go higher *(Joshua 1:8)*

Receive God's Word. God's Word will give me God's thoughts God's thoughts will give me God's ways God's ways will make me prosper.

When you have the mind of Christ, you can be sober, clear thinking or else the Bible says you are a drunkard walking off balance in everything you do. *(Luke 21:34, Romans 13:13)* You must be steadfast, unmovable, always abiding in the word of God. The Bible says Jesus promised that if you abide in Him and His words abide in you, you may ask for what you will and He will give it to you. *(John 15:7)* Also, we have this confidence that if we pray anything according to the word of God that He will hear us, and do as we ask Him.

(1 John 5:14-15)

God is able to perform His word. *(Romans 4:21)* We must also learn to speak His word because God's word will never return to Him void. It will accomplish what He pleases and will prosper where He sends it. *(Isaiah 55:11)* We must speak God's word because the angels hearken to the word of God. *(Psalms 103:20)* Also, the word of God is a lamp to your feet and a light to your pathway *(Psalm 119:105)*. Anytime God is going to do something in your life, He is going to give you His word because in the beginning was the word, and it was the spoken word that produced life.

The word is our peace because we believe and trust and know with full assurance that the word will do what it says because God cannot lie. *(Numbers 23:19)* The word is our breakthrough; it breaks down barricades because what can stand up to the truth? The word brings joy because when you know you are living right you can be happy and you are blessed wherever you go because you take the Blesser with you when you have the word. The

Advocate is Jesus. Jesus is the Word and the word of God will produce something in you and for you because God is a creator and He is creating you to be His masterpiece. *(John 1:1, 3)*

When a soldier is in the midst of a battle, he keeps his weapon close to him and he is ready to use it to attack. Our weapons are not carnal (flesh thinking), but mighty to the pulling down of strongholds. *(2 Corinthians 10:4)* As you move, God is moving for you and the battle is not yours, but God's.

(2 Chronicles 20:15) God is going to win the battle through you. That's why you must exhaust every avenue the enemy is trying to attack and cut it down with the word which is your sword. *(Ephesians 6:17)* Keep the word near you because that's the weapon you are going to need to win. David was a mighty warrior, and he was a man after God's own heart. He understood about spiritual warfare and he utilized everything God gave him to win. He recognized he was a man. He prayed, he repented, he danced and praised God in the midst of all hell, and he died an honorable man. He let God be the truth and every other man a liar.

We need to seek first the kingdom of God and His righteousness, and all things shall be added to us. *Matthew 6:33)* Seek God's will, and the right way He said to respond to the attacks of the devil, and He will give you the grace to stand and instruct you all the way. You will pass your test and have a testimony. Then you can begin to share your story on how you fought the good fight of faith because every true soldier will have a war story.

God wants us to walk in our revelation and not in our circumstances. We are complete in _Jesus. We move, live, and have our being in Him. *(Acts 17:28)*

Fire is the necessary ingredient when God begins to process you for greatness. When you cry out to God to go higher, what you are really saying is more fire.

Chapter Five

Fire Proof

Fire is the heat that is necessary to burn off the flesh. After we have studied the word of God and we have increased in wisdom and knowledge, we have to know that the Bible says: *"Every man's work will be tested by fire". (1 Corinthians 3:13)*

It is easy to say, "I am a Christian, I believe in God" when all is well and your needs are met. The question is, how are you going to respond to God and what is your behavior going to be like when you don't know how your needs are going to be met and all the people you relied on seem to have turned their backs on you, and you are not on top anymore? The fire then will test your character to see if you really believe what you preach. The fire will take you away from carnal thinking because when you are in the fire, the fire's purpose is to help you seek God's face for everything.

God is actually training you on how to trust Him for all your provision because as long as we have the necessary means to live we still feel in control. But what happens when you are laid off that job and now there is no income? This is a good situation to know that God is your source. It's only when you decrease that God can increase in your life, and you will see He can provide for you and your family because he is your Jehovah Jireh, your provider.

The fire is a refiner and a purifier. God said for us to be holy because He is holy. That requires us to live right and walk upright and apply His word to our situations and circumstances. God wants us to get in agreement with His word. He says, *'This day I give you daily bread."* Matthew 6:11, Luke 11:3)

Too many times we walk in that which we know, in what we see, and we are overcome and consumed with fear because we don't understand how we are going to achieve or accomplish our goals, and how we are going to provide for our needs. It seems like you can hardly make it. This is a time when you feel frustrated, depressed, and don't know what to do, and it seems like God has forsaken you. The purpose of the fire is to help you to realize that you need God, and to show you your dependency on the Lord.

The Lord has enabling power that will give you the strength to do what you never thought you could do. The more inadequate you feel is a sign of you decreasing which gives the Holy Spirit the ability to increase. He says, *"When you are weak that is when I will be strong".* (2 Corinthians 12:9)

Our storms are necessary to heal us from past hurts, unforgiveness, and they strengthen the gifts and talents that have already been deposited on the inside of us.

God wants to equip you to fulfill your purpose and to increase your faith, because we go from faith to faith and glory to glory. The more you can trust the Lord, the more He is able to move for you in every situation. God desires to bless His people and He says, *'When I come, will I find faith?" (Luke 18:8)* When God desires to show you His goodness or His glory, it's going to require faith on your part. The just ought to live by faith. Whatever you profess and whatever you believe is what you are going to have to live by.

We all know the term "talk is cheap, and action speaks louder than words". Faith without works is dead, and you are going to have to put the word in action to get your breakthrough. *Games 2:20, 26)* It's that simple. Your faith is going to have to be presented in the way you live because sometimes that's the best witness people need to see, and a way to honor God.

Although we may not physically see Him in the natural, but in the spirit God is our heavenly Father. He is watching over us, and He loves us dearly. He has promised that He would teach us His ways. When we submit our will to God and begin to seek God's wisdom and God's heart on what we need to do to succeed; then we have allowed God a place to perform on our behalf because He is *an ever present help in trouble". (Psalm 46:1)*

We have to learn how to wait on God because when God is working on your situation He is not in a hurry. God will lead you by the hand and take you through, step by step, because God is not going to leave you the same way

He found you. He wants you to grow into maturity where you can be called a Son of God, walking after the spirit. God knows you and He can handle your storm. He created you, and He has allowed you to be faced with this situation. Just know if He brought you to it, He can bring you through it. He said that He would not put more on you than you can bear. Troubles don't last always. The fire is just an opportunity that God has given you to take the word and apply it to each circumstance. You have to pass your test in order to have a testimony.

Trust the Word, and you will see He will make a way for you. God knows a million ways to bless you, but He will prepare you for the blessing because not only does He want to see you blessed, but also He wants you to be a blessing. So seek those things which are above before you seek those things in the world. That is the first indication that you are operating with a renewed mind. A faith mind.

Keep trusting the Lord even when you can't see Him because God knows your limitations and He knows what will motivate you. When your breakthrough comes it's going to be by you knowing God, His spirit, and His voice. This is just a tip; the very thing you believe God to do is going to require trusting the God you know. The God that has always been with you. The God that has always showed up at the right time. The vessel that God chooses to use to bring you out, you may not be familiar with or believe God would operate through. He will use this vessel to humble and break you as well as bless you.

Remember He said, *"the wealth of the wicked is laid up for the just" .(Proverbs 1.3:22)* As God makes this transfer, He is expecting you to abide in Him, believe and trust Him for the provision, and not look at or judge the vessel. Remember God has called you to be a light in dark places, and the salt of the earth. *Matthew 5:13-14)* God is leading you to people that do not know Him, and blessing you through your obedience to Him.

God wants us to learn certain principles, like
"take no thought for your life, what you shall eat, or what you shall drink; or for your body, what you shall put on because your father in heaven knows you have need of all these things."
Matthew 6:25-32) "God shall supply all your needs according to his riches in glory by Christ Jesus." (Philippians 4:19)

Also, the fire is designed to stretch your faith because you cannot please God without faith. It's easy to trust God when you can clearly see a way out of a situation, but what happens when your livelihood is tested and you don't have any means to pay your rent, feed your children, all your possessions are lost, and the people you love are gone? This is another opportunity to see what your house and your character is built on. The Bible says,

"That the house built on the rock
(which is the word of God) will stand" (Luke 6:48)

His grace is sufficient for you, and He is able to keep you in the midst of every situation. No man is exempt from the fire. Either someone is just going in, or right in the middle of the fire, or just coming out.

Sometimes we do not understand why we seem to have to endure one storm after another - so many fire conditions all at the same time. I want you to be encouraged and know that God said His word is alive. So if God's word is alive then you have to live it out. If He said, *"you are more than conquerors", then you have to have something to conquer. (Romans 8:37)* If He said you are above and not beneath, than you have to have something to stick your head up and above. So that is why God wants us to have the mind of Christ. Believe what God said, do it just like He says to do it, and you will walk into the miracle God has just for you - a blessing with your name on it.

We need to understand that trials and tribulation don't come to tear you down, but they are designed to produce patience, experience, and hope in our Creator. Jesus said

PROPHECY:

Let the Lord bring you through. It's the 'Ford of God that is going to transform you and resurrect your mind to go higher. Jesus promised that your blessing is on the other side of through. The rain will fall from heaven. The former and the latter rain. God will bring you into a good land. A land flowing with milk and honey because of, your faith and obedience.

So know that your labor is not in vain. As you decrease, the God that's in you can increase. As you begin to follow after the Spirit, you are walking in your destiny and know that promotion comes from the Lord.

So look up and trust His guidance because He will never fail you. He loves you too much, and He wants to bless you. You have to come to in your faith where you know, and trust the Lord regardless of what you see, but trust in that which you know. That which has been revealed to you by your spirit. Follow peace, and it will lead you all the way.

Chapter Six

Arise

After being defeated and living a life with very little victory. I thank God for teaching me His principles and learning how to speak the word of God in distressful, mind-boggling, and impossible situations. He who is in you is greater than He who is in the world. Jesus has given you permission to take authority.

Arise, Arise, Arise, I want you to go with me into that place of God's peace that passes all understanding. That just simply means you have to come up a little bit in your faith. You have to trust God even though you cannot see Him because He is always near.

When you get into that place which is the presence of God, you will receive His joy that's unspeakable. The fact is you can't get there if you are worried about not having enough money to pay your bills, are burden down with the cares of this world. Frustrated with your supervisor on that job, are contemplating a divorce because of an aggravation in your marriage. You may even be ready to give up on that rebellious child that just don't seem to act right. I know all about losing all your hope and I know how you sometimes just keep on doubting. I know what the doctor said, but the truth of the matter is whose report are you going to believe. God said, *"kg aside every weight that so easily beset you" (Hebrews 12:1)* because we serve and all seeing and an all knowing God who sits up high and looks down low. The earth has no sorrow that heaven cannot heal.

So I release God's healing virtue into your life, into your home, into your job, in that hospital room, in your finances, in your mind, and be made whole in the name of Jesus. The Lord's presence is with you, and you can make it with Jesus. He will see you through.

So let this be your day to lift up the King of Kings and the Lord of Lords because He is the lifter of your head. *(Psalms 3:3)* So I call you into that new life which is in Jesus Christ, and I say to you today to arise, arise, arise.

It's time to stop all the bickering and complaining for your light has come. *(Isaiah 60:1)* Look about yourself and see all that God has given you, and know that you have the victory. The battle has already been won. So I want you today to arise, arise, arise because you will no longer be defeated, and the Lord has given his angels charge over you. *(Psalms 91:11)* By Jesus stripes you have already been healed. Just receive it.

Shout out loud in the devil's face. I will not die, but live to declare the Glory of God. Sometimes we just have to encourage ourselves in the Lord, and repent from all the doubting. You must know that God is still on the throne. God sent his Son Jesus who shed his blood, and paid our sin debt. Shout, I am free and you can live because Jesus lives. God has chosen you, and you are a part of His Holy family. *(Exodus 19:6)*

If God is for you, who can be against you? There is not a battle that God can ever lose because He is God. Whatever God says IS, and whatever God wants to be will BE. Who is able to stand against the Almighty? He is your deliverer, He is your refuge, He is a strong tower, He is a way maker, He is a lamp to your feet and a light to your path, He is the bright and morning star, He is a lily in the valley, and He is the good Sheppard. So keep your hand in the Master's hand, and arise, arise, arise.

I decree to you today that you have access into God's divine favor. *(Romans 5:2)* This favor will provide for everything you need, this favor will open doors for you. You have already been equipped with all spiritual blessings. When Jesus died on the cross and said, "It is finished," every provision that you will ever need was set in place. Just get in line with God and His word. Let God's peace lead you and receive the joy of His salvation. *(Isaiah 55:12)*

Keeping this in mind, you can arise, arise, arise. Your blessing is in the pressing. *(Philippians14)* Faith comes by hearing the preached Word of God. Ask God to lead you to a Sheppard that is preaching the true Word of God, and begin to let the true word of God rise up on the inside of you because all things are possible if you would just believe. *(Mark 9:23)* While you are trying to figure out how you are going to get out of a crisis or a bad situation, God has already worked it out. Jesus came that you might have life and have it more abundantly.

Arise, and shine. Put the devil in his place, and that's up under your feet. Begin to shoot arrows back at the enemy by speaking God's words, and take authority. Confess the word of God, and know that you have what you shall say: *(Romans 10:10)*

- I am the righteousness of God
- I have been redeemed from poverty, sickness, and sin.
- I can do all things through Jesus Christ that strengthens me.
- I am a tree planted by the rivers of water, and whatever I do shall prosper.
- God is working all things out for my good.
- Great is He that's in me
- All the fruits of the spirit are working on the inside of me.
- The joy of the Lord is my strength
- God Is my refuge, my fortress, in whom I trust
- God is my provider
- I am a blessing wherever I go.
- No weapon formed against me shall prosper.
- Wealth and riches are in my house.
- I have the favor of God
- I am His beloved and the apple of His eyes.
- All my sins have been forgiven.
- I walk by faith and not by sight.
- I am not moved by what I see.
- I have been delivered from the powers of darkness

Arise, arise, arise, and know that you will come forth as pure gold because If *any man be in Christ, he is a new creature: old things are passed away, behold all things are become new" (2 Corinthians 5:17)* Just receive it.

It's a new day. Let God be glorified in the new you.

Prophecy:

Soldiers, it's time to line up because it's time to arise. I decree that this is a divine order day.
God's presence is with you and He will never leave you nor forsake you.

God wants to heal you. God wants to heal your finances, He wants to heal your marriage, He wants to heal your body, He wants to heal, deliver; and save your soul. He wants you to be made whole. He has the Power to raise you up from that place of depression, oppression, poverty, loneliness, and fear. So I break and I bind all the curses of darkness over your life by the Power and blood of Jesus Christ and I loose God's spiritual healing today.

This is a day of rejoicing, a day of a renewed mind, It's a day of a breakthrough, a day of coming fourth.
It's available to you.

God wants you today to Arise, Arise, Arise because you have a right to the tree of life. So receive it by Faith.

Chapter Seven

Healing

God is a Healer, and earth has no sorrow that heaven cannot heal. God wants you to know that He created your body, and He created it to be the temple where the Holy spirit will live inside of you.

'What? Know ye not that your body is the temple of the Holy Ghost which is in you, which ye have of God, and ye are not your own?"
(1 Corinthians 6:19)

God does not want anyone sick or afflicted with pain. We are responsible for the way we treat our bodies and sometimes we take our health for granted by eating poorly, and putting different types of drugs or alcohol into our body. Often, we have different sex partners which have caused us to be afflicted with a venereal disease. Some have been physically and mentally abused in relationships. Some bodily injuries occur by unforeseen accidents or illnesses. Regardless of the situation or circumstances, sickness has caused more people pain and unhappiness.

Jesus has the remedy for this: He said, If *any among you that are sick, let him pray". (James 5:14-15)*

Jesus wants you to talk to him about your ailment because *bore our sickness and cured all our diseases and by His stripes you are healed". Isaiah (53:4-5)*

This means that the sickness or ailment that you are attacked with does not belong to you because Jesus redeemed you from the curse. So give your sickness to the one who paid for your health which is Jesus.

This is a powerful statement because Jesus is a Healer. He paid the price, and took on the sins and the curses that have been afflicted on mankind which gives you the right to healing.

There are many stories in the Bible that testify to the fact that Jesus is a Healer. Here are few:

Blind Bartimaeus receives his sight (St. Mark 10:46)

Blind Bartimaeus was a begger who sat on the side of the road. He heard that Jesus was passing by from the crowd that was following Jesus. Jesus had performed many miracles in the land, and blind Bartimaeus cried out loud as Jesus was passing by hoping that he could get Jesus' attention, and receive his site.

The crowd tried to quiet the blind man from crying out to Jesus, but he continued yelling out loud "Thou son of David, have mercy on me" as Jesus walked by. When Jesus heard his sincere cry for help, he had compassion. Jesus said, "What wilt thou that I should do unto thee? The blind man said unto him, Lord, that I might receive my sight. Jesus said, *"Go thy way; thy faith bath made thee whole."(St. Mark 10:52)*

The blind man immediately gained his site.
This man had faith that he could be healed from his illness of being born blind. Even though the crowd of people try to quiet him down, blind Bartimaeus did not let that discourage him. The blind man was persistent to gain Jesus attention.

Blind Bartimaeus called on the name of Jesus, and he received his miracle. He no longer walked in darkness, but he came into the marvelous light. When you cry out to Jesus, He will hear your cry, and will answer you.
'Then shalt thou call, and the Lord shall answer; thou shalt cry, and He shall say, Here I am.
(Isaiah 58:9)

Women who touch the hem of Jesus garment and was made whole. (Mathew 9:20-22)

There was a woman who had a bleeding condition for 12 long years. She had spent all her money trying to pay the doctors for her healing. There seemed to be no cure for her. Her situation was hopeless. She heard that
Jesus was in her town passing by. She had to make a decision to believe in Jesus even after all the bad reports

she had got from the doctors, and after all the medicine she had taken. She had to believe that Jesus was not like the other physicians, but that Jesus was the great physician where there is nothing impossible with God.

Tut Jesus beheld them, and said unto them, with men this is impossible; but with God all things are possible." Mathew 19:26)

So as Jesus passed by with the crowds that were surrounding him, she pressed her way through the crowd and humbled herself. She had a dying faith that if she could just touch the hem of Jesus garment some kind of way, she could be healed. When the women got close enough to reach out, and touch the hem of Jesus garment, instantaneously, she received her miracle. She was made whole.

Jesus recognized the lady's faith, and how she was willing to humble herself and press her way through the crowd to touch him because she believe he could heal her.

Jesus told the women that her *FAITH IN JESUS* is what made her whole. The bleeding stop and she walked in total healing. Mentally, financially, and physically.

Lame man at the pool gets his healing. (John 5:1)

There was a man at the pool called Bethesda, and at the pool laid many sick and lame people. There was a man who had been there 38 years in a sick condition, and needed healing.

The man had all types of excuses that cause him not to get healed or get in the pool. He said, too many people would get in the pool before him, and he had no one to assist him in getting in the pool. The lame man knew at a certain time of the year that an angel would be sent to heal those that was able to make it into the pool.

Jesus knew that the lame man was hurt, frustrated, and very determine to be healed. The man being lame was without help, and without anyone caring to assist him. Jesus asked him a question? He said, do you want to be made whole? The man answered, yes, and Jesus healed him that minute. The lame man was able to pick up his colt that he laid lame on, and put it up under his arm. The man for the first time got up and walked.

All three of these stories have one thing in common, Jesus cared for those that was sick, and He had a day of healing prepared for each one.

He passed by where they were sick and afflicted. Each person touched Jesus with their Faith because they were willing to bring their sickness, and situation to Jesus no matter how impossible the situation appeared to be. They went against the obstacles that try to prevent them from being healed. They trusted and believed that Jesus had the power to heal them. All three of these people had the Faith and determination to call on Jesus, and reach out to Jesus when they saw and believe Him to be the Healer, and they all three got HEALED.

God is no respecter of person. What he did for those people who believed He could heal them. He will do the same for you. God specializes in things, situations, conditions, and people that seem impossible. So if you are sick and afflicted. Pray and talk to Jesus. Trust and believe, and let him cure you of all your diseases.

'Who forgiveth all thine iniquities; and who healeth all thy diseases." (Psalms 103:3)

Prophecy:

I degree and declare that this is the acceptable year of the Lord. I degree and declare that Jesus is a Healer, and He will heal you of all your infirmities. I cover you in the blood of Jesus Christ, and take authority, and declare by His stripes you are healed (Isaiah 53:5). He carried your sickness and bore your diseases, and He redeemed you from every curse. Cast your cares on Jesus and be HEALED, and be set free in your mind, body, and soul. Be made WI-10T .F. If Jesus sets you free than you are free indeed. I bind that spirit of infirmity, and I lose the anointing which destroy burdening and yokes, and I say to you today. "be Healed in Jesus Name!"

The Lord is in this place, and His glory shall fill your temple and wash away all your pain, misery, and afflictions. In Jesus name.

Chapter Eight

Prayer

*'Don't worry about anything, but pray about everything."
(Philippians 4.6)*

Jesus is on the mainline and you can call him up, and tell him what you want. Prayer is communicating with God, and Jesus is only a prayer away.

Much Prayer, Much Power , Little Prayer, Little Power, No Prayer, No Power

Prayer is simply man talking with God. As we pray, we learn how to put our Faith in God to bring our petitions, and needs before the Lord so that we may be filled with his Peace, and an Abundant life.
am come that they might have lift, and that they might have it more abundantly." John 10:10)

Prayer is not granted to any particular denomination or respect of person. Prayer is available to anyone who will put their faith and trust in Jesus to believe him to be the sovereign God. Little do we know that God wants to know what is on your mind, what is in your heart, and he wants to heal you from everything that causes you pain, suffering, and sorrow.

God has the power to fix everything and every situation. Jesus is only a prayer away, and He is a present help in the time of trouble.

"God is our refuge and strength, a very present help in trouble." (Psalms 46:1)

God can do all things except fail. Sometimes we think it is so hard to get in touch with God because we feel that our circumstances are impossible for God to handle.

There are many reasons why we don't pray to God and some may even feel that because they are living a life of sin or have forgiveness in their heart that there is no use in praying. Many have unhealed hurts, and do not want to talk to God because deep down inside we may feel bitter or think we are not worthy of God's help. That's the biggest lie of the Devil. Jesus died and gave you access through the blood to come boldly to the throne of Grace. *'Let us therefore come boldly unto the throne of grace, that we may obtain mercy, and find grace to help in time of need" (Hebrews 4:16).*

There are so many obstacles, circumstances, and distractions that cause us not to pray. It takes belief and faith in Jesus to get your prayers answered. Jesus said,*' If you pray and believe you shall receive." (I/I ark 11:24)*

One of the reasons we feel challenged to pray is because we never really tried to talk to God because the world always seem to offer us so much advise through talk shows, success magazines, and we listen to friends and other people testimony's. We don't rely on God at all until our situation becomes impossible where there is no one who can help in the time of need. When the situation gets too hard for you, that's when you have to know it is perfect for God.

"Is anything to hard for God" (Genesis 18:14)

Hard times and impossible situations is the place God will bring us to a lot of times because He wants to talk to us. God knows that when we are in trouble, and faced with all types of crises, and fiery trials that will be the time we will pray and give God our attention.

God has the answers for every situation you can possible face or go through. If God brought you to it, He is able to bring you through it.

Now that you may have a desire to pray, you may have some questions on how to pray:

How should we begin our prayer?

God is a Holy God and He has instructed us to come boldly to the Throne of Grace. *lie said enter into his gates with Thanksgiving and His courts with praise. Be thankful unto Him, and bless His name." (Psalms 100:4)* God wants to first know that you are thankful for whom He is, and that you are thankful for what He has already done in your life all the way up to this point in your life. Next, He said to enter His courts with praise. This means to come into

His presence singing and rejoicing, and marveling over God's awesomeness. This shows God that you are excited that you have the victory in Jesus.

Once you have entered into that place that you are thankful and rejoicing for the good things that God has done, now bring your petition and request to God with a sincere heart. God already knows what is going on in your life, what happened, what's in your heart, and Jesus can help.

So lay your burdens down on Jesus, and tell Him from the smallest to the biggest concerns, problems, or situations you have.

"Cast thy burden loon the Lord, and He shall sustain thee: He shall never suffer the righteous to be moved."
(Psalms 55:22)

Next, take your faith which may be the size of a mustard seed, and trust God to be bigger than your problem. Then you will know that God is not like man. What you tell God in secret, He will not tell no one else. He said, find a closet or a secret place, and talk your heart out to God because that is the sacrifice that God is looking for and is welcome at his Altar.

The sacrifices of God are a broken spirit: a broken and contrite heart. 0 God thou wilt not despise. (Psalms 51:17)

The Lord will perfect that which concerns me. (Psalms 138:8)

When you pray, it brings great comfort to know that God is listening to our prayers. He hears the prayers of the righteous.

"we have confidents that if we pray anything according to His will, He will hear us, and do what we ask "(1 John 5:14-15)

It is God's will that we talk to him through prayer. The bible tells us to *"pray without ceasing"* *(1 Thessalonians 5:17.)*

Jesus also states that whosoever would call on the Lord, He shall hear them. God sits up high, but He looks down low. God never sleeps nor slumber. God already had the answer before you prayed, and He was just waiting on you to seek him so that He could show you that He was available all the time. While you are trying to figure it out, God had already worked it out. He said, what you pray in secret, He will reward you openly.

"When thou prayest, enter into thy closet, and when thou hast shut till door, pray to the Father which is in secret; and thy father which seeth in secret shall reward thee openly." (Matthew 6:6)

When you are praying to God, the Devil will send two agents your way called doubt and disbelief. He will try to allow negative people to speak to you regarding your situation to cause you to fear and doubt God. So when you pray and can't see the answer or have the slightest idea how God is going to answer your prayers; continue to keep the Faith because without Faith you cannot please God. Faith takes you into a realm that goes beyond your understanding. So don't try to figure it out. Just know God is working it out.

Let your requests be made known unto God, and the peace of God which passeth all understanding, shall keep your hearts and minds through Christ Jesus." (Philippians 4:6-7)

Always remember that a delay is not a denial. You cannot hurry God. He may not come when you want him, but He is always on time.

'He shall call upon me, and I will answer him: I will be with him in trouble; I will deliver him, and honour him." *(Psalms 91:15)* So take courage, and keep the Faith. Always remember to pray without ceasing because much prayer brings about much power from on high.

Whether you know it or not you have a part to play in getting your prayers answer. Your part is to trust God and know that He is faithful even when we lose heart and give up. God is never caught off guard and He is still in charge. We need to call those things which be not as though they are, and say out of our mouth what you believe God will do for you. This is a great sign of faith and it is always good to encourage yourself while you are waiting on your answered prayer. Read inspirational books and talk to people that have faith.

It is also powerful to come together with other believers in prayer. God said, *"If any two or three come together I will be in the midst."*
(Mathew 18:19-20.)

Also sometimes because of the intensity of the storm or circumstance you need others to assist you in getting a prayer through, and always pray consistently. Because we ought to bear the burdens of others.

Hear ye one another's burdens, and so fulfill the law of Christ" (Galatians 6:2)

'There is great strength when we come together in unity t o pray." (Psalms 133.1)

'The effectual fervent prayer of the righteous man availeth much. "Games 5:16).

This just simple mean that if you believe and have faith in Jesus, God had declared you righteous and your prayers are welcomed in heaven. His power will produce change and give you the results you desire.
He said, *"you delight yourself in him, he will give you the desires of your heart. (Psalms 37:4)*

I thank God always for his Mercy because He loves us so much and He knows what we need and what is necessary to get us through our test. No test, no testimony, and no promotion.

'Promotion comes from the Lord" (Psalms 75:6)

Even though you may not be in the habit of praying or just in the beginning stages of your prayer life or you may even be an ordain minister who prays all the time; God had divinely given us a prayer to pray each day:

Our Father, which art in Heaven. Hallow be thy name. Thy Kingdom come, thy will be done, on earth as it is in heaven . Give us this day, our daily bread, and forgive us our debt as we forgive our debtor. Lead us not into temptation, but deliver us from evil. For thy is the kingdom, and the power, and the glory, forever and ever. Amen.

This prayer starts off by acknowledging God as a Father and His dwelling place which is in Heaven and the Power in His name. The prayer also announces God's plan to establish His kingdom on earth in the same order that he operates from heaven. He allows us to pray that he supply our need and walk in forgiveness as he has paid the price for the forgiveness of our sins. He divinely protects us from the enemy. He also closes the prayer out with His kingdom will always stand, and He has the power at all times to sustain your life, and He deserves all the Glory. Now and forever. Amen. (which simple means to agree)

"The footsteps of the righteous man are ordered by God
"(Psalms 119.133.)

If you feel like you have gotten off course or your right in the middle of a storm, you must know that you are not the first, the last, or the only one. Either someone is just going into a storm, is right in the middle of a storm, or coming out of a storm. All you have to do is get back on course and acknowledge that you need God's help in prayer. He said,

"Look to His hill which cometh your help because al/your help comes from the Lord" (Psalms 121.1)

'Trust in the Lord with all your heart; and lean not unto thine own understanding. In all thy i.v6c acknowledge him, and he shall direct thy paths." (Proverbs 3:5)

Praying to God is great, but your prayer will not get answer unless you pray, In The name of Jesus. Jesus is the mediator between man and God, and it was His blood that was shed which gave you access to come

boldly to the throne to lay your petitions before God. Jesus is the one interceding for us and all our prayers have to be presented to God, In Jesus name.

"Where you have ask nothing in my name."
John 15:16).

"If you should ask any thing in my name, I will do it"

John 14:13-14)

You can't get to the father except by Jesus.

The type of prayers that get answered are prayers that are:

- Prayed in the name of Jesus
- Prayers that are prayed according to God's word,
- prayers that are asked with the right motive
- prayers that are prayed with faith.

Prayers that don't get answered are:
- prayers that have evil motives.
- Prayers that are prayed with unforgiveness in your heart.

God is a good God, and he wants us to pray with a good heart. God sent Jesus to forgive us of our sins and likewise He wants us to be willing to forgive others as well.

"Be ye kind one to another, tender hearted, forgiving one another, even as God for Christ's sake has forgiven you." (Ephesians 4:32) A delay is not a denial. Sometimes God has to prepare us for our blessing so that when He bless us, we can be a blessing to others and those in our family, and to people we interact with every day. So sometimes God has to mold and shape us as well as stretch, and break us, and Increase our Faith in Him before He can answer our prayers. We should always pray consistently and with Faith. Our Prayers should always be motivated with a

sincere heart. Our prayers bring God's power, plan, protection, and abundant provision into our life.

'Hearken unto the voice of my cry, my King, and my God: for unto thee will I pray. My voice shalt thou hear in the morning, 0 Lord; in the morning will I direct my prayer unto thee, and will look up." (Psalms 5:2-3)

Chapter Nine

Your change has come

Trouble doesn't last always. There is a blessing on the other side of through. If God brought you to it, He will surely bring you through it.

"So, Arise and shine for your light has come, and the Glory of God has risen upon you."
(Isaiah 60:1)

No man can arise without light. The light is the wisdom of God. So no matter what circumstances you are facing or what has taken place in your life, if you desire to be free and come out of your captivity; you are going to need the wisdom of God. The wisdom of God is His Word.

When you get the Word of God on the inside of you, you can become all of what God would have you to be, and go where God leads you. The light will be turned on because you are now being led by the Holy Spirit. God's thoughts are so much higher than our thoughts. *(Isaiah 55:9)*

God's thoughts will bring us out of our captivity, and change will begin to take place in our lives the moment the word of God gets rooted in our spirit.

The glory of God is his goodness. So when you yield your life to God, and begin to do things God's way, and seek to please him;

He said, "there Is no good thing that I will withhold from him."
Palms 84:11)

You will receive favor from the Lord. So what God Is saying to you today, if you want your situation or circumstances to change, you are going to have to get into His Word. Jesus said, "this book of the law shall not depart out of thy mouth; but thou shalt meditate on it day and night, that you may observe and do according to all that is written in it. For then you shall make your way prosperous, and then you shall deal wisely and have good success." (Joshua 1:8).

See, God is trying to get our mind set to change. You have to let the mind of Christ be in you. The mind of Christ is developed by reading your word, praying, and listening for God's guidance through the Holy Spirit.

So we have to begin to build up our faith. The only way we can do that is to exercise the Word by putting it into action which is simply applying it to our life circumstances and situations. That's the only way you are going to see God's manifestation of His Word because He is faithful to perform it. God must have thought Faith was important because He said we cannot please him without it. *"But without faith it is impossible to please and be satisfactory to Him. For whoever*

71

would come near to God must believe that God exists and that He is the rewarder of those who earnestly and diligently seek Him." (Hebrews 11:6)

See Faith sees like God sees. Faith goes beyond your natural site. When you can't see a way out or don't know how you are going to make it, faith will take you into the supernatural realm where God now steps in, and begin to perform a miracle in your life. That' why God said, *'The Just must live by Faith'. (Galatians 3:11)* Because faith takes you into the realm of the impossible and that's where God does his best work so that He will get the glory.

So when you begin to get the mind of Christ, you will believe what God says about you in His Word. Site is your circumstances, and your limitations. God wants you to operate in faith so He can take you beyond your limitations and bring you into what eyes have not seen or ears heard.

"For since the beginning of the world men have not heard, nor perceived by the ear, neither hath the eye seen, 0 God, beside thee, what he bath prepared for him that waiteth for him."
(Isaiah 64:4)

You have to get in agreement with God's Word. God has chosen a people for himself, and He knows us by name and He called us to walk in the spirit by *"Every Word that preceeded out the mouth of God"*
(Deuteronomy 8:3).

God is calling us to obedience. He wants us to see as He sees and to go where He directs us, and to say what He tells us to say, and do what His Word tells us to do. That is the only way we are going to develop the character of God, and have the confidence in our maker, and be all that God intended for us to be. It is going to require faith. If you was to cut God, He would bleed Faith. Faith takes you out of your normal thinking and brings you into God's supernatural blessing. So the only way to grow in Faith is to be a doer of the Word, and not just a hearer because God is able to perform His Word. When you apply the Word of God to your life, you will see the promises of God manifest every time in your life circumstances because He said,

"His Word will not return to him void, and it 2vill prosper in the place that he sent it". (Isaiah 55:11)

When you receive the Word in your heart, and it takes root, you will produce a 30, 60, and 100 fold harvest. No man can say he doesn't have faith because every man has been given a measure of Faith. *(Romans 12:3).* Faith helps you fulfill God's will and God's perfect plan for your life. You have to submit yourself to God and His Lordship, and become like putty in his hand.

'Be not conformed to this world: but be transformed by the renewing of your mind, that ye may prove what is that good, and acceptable, and perfect will of God" (Romans 12:1)

When you surrender your will to the Lord you will experience his goodness and mercy in your life because God operates through faith, and faith is forsaken all I trust him. God can be trusted because He is a God that cannot lie, and He is a father that never sleeps are slumber. His eyes are on the sparrow at all times.

Faith is developed by praying, studying the Word of God, and listening to the preached Word.

"So then faith cometh by hearing, and healing by the Word of God" (Romans 10:17)

Let God take you through the process of resurrecting your life that he may impart and implant new life into you through His spirit which gives life, and produces the Love of God on the inside of you which comes through abiding in Christ through Faith that He is God.

"He that abideth in me, and I in him, the same bringeth forth much fruit: for without me ye can do nothing". (John 15:5).

See we are transformed by truth and trouble. God's word is the Truth and trouble is designed to help us develop our testimony to bring glory to God. No test, no testimony.
Jesus said *"In this world you will have trouble, but be of a good cheer for I have overcome the world' (John 16:33)*

The devil tempts you to destroy you, and God test you to promote you. So when you are in pain and all is not well, Jesus will help you overcome it because he sent you a comforter which is the Holy Spirit.

"But the comforter, which is the Holy Ghost, whom the Father will send in my name, he shall teach you all things, and bring all things to your remembrance, whatsoever I have said unto you. (John 14:26) `He will be a present help in trouble.
"(Psalms 46:1)

This scripture lets you know that Jesus can handle your situation because He is a burden bearer, a mountain mover, and more than able to do exceeding, abundantly, above all that we ask or think, according to the power that worketh in us. *(Ephesians 3:20).*

He said, if you have the faith the size of a mustard seed you can move a mountain. God has given us the formula for change: He said to call those things which are not as though they were.

'Now Faith is the substance of things hoped for, the evidence of things not seen." (Hebrews 11:1)

Just simple say what God says, and the angels of heaven are standing by hearkening to the Word of God to bring it to past.

"The words were heard, and I am come for thy words" (Daniel
10:12)

Now when you are operating in Faith which is believing
God and taking Him at His Word, The Devil is going to
try to steal the Word that God is sowing into your heart
because He knows if it takes root you will make him
out to be the liar that He is, and develop a testimony
which will glorify God. So the Devil is always trying to
cause you to fear, but God did not give you that spirit of
fear. That spirit of fear comes from the Devil.

*'For God bath not given us the Spirit of fear; but of power,
and of love, and a sound mind"*
(2 Timothy 1:7),

When you begin to operate in fear that keeps a curse on
your life because it hinders your progress and stagnates
your ability to perform and walk in the promises of God.
So if you want to experience a change in your life, you
have to find the Snake in your situation. Its real simple:
Let's look at the word *CURSE,* and in the middle of the
word curse is a big S, and when you take out that big S
you will get the word *CURE.* So the same is in your
situation. When you find the snake or the root which is
the cause of your problem and get rid of it, you can get
your break through. Jesus came to give you peace and expected end.

'For *I know the thoughts that I think toward you, saith the Lord,
thoughts of peace, and not of evil, to give you an expected end"
(Jeremiah 29:11)*

God has more for you, but you are not going to enjoy
your salvation without feasting on the word daily. God
never intended that anyone stay the same. He said, come
as you are because He was going to make the change in
your life.

*Therefore if any man be in Christ, He is a new creature: old
things are passed away; behold, all things are become new, (2
Corinthians 5:17)*

The only person that likes change is a baby, and change
brings us out of our comfort zone. God wants to make an
exchange with you today. If you are sad, God wants to
give you Joy. If you are fearful, God wants you to
become faithful. If you are depressed, God wants you to
lift up your head. If you feel defeated, God gave you the
victory. If you are sick, God is a Healer. He paid the
price that you may have life and have it more
abundantly. You have a right to the tree of life, and all
things are possible if you would believe God, and
believe His Word. He said, trust in God, but also trust in
Jesus.

*"Let not your heart not be troubled: ye believe in God,
believe also in me. "(John 14:1)*

77

Here is my testimony of Faith to encourage your heart that there is nothing impossible with God.

Walking out on the Word (testimony)

We often hear all kinds of Biblical testimonies on Faith, but I would like to share my testimony on how I walked on the Word and received the miracle God had for me:

I was faced with an eviction, and threatened to be put out of my home that I had lived in for two years because I had been laid off my job. I had no income whatsoever and no one to rely on to help me pay my rent, and provide for my three kids that were at the house. The courts had given me seven days to evacuate the premises, and I had previous evictions so I knew it would be hard for me to find another apartment right away. I had no money to move, and I did not know what to do. I prayed and put my trust in Jesus. Jesus, spoke this word to me all through the situation. *"Be still, and know that I am God" (Psalms 46:10)*

It was real hard for me to be still when my whole life was about to fall apart, and my situation was hopeless. I cried many nights, and I wished the situation would just go away, but it never did. I fasted and kept thanking God for what he was going to do even though I could not even imagine how he was going to fix my situation. I just knew I needed to be obedient, and believe God. I remained still in the process of the marshals coming to evict me the next couple of days. I believed if I had packed one bag that it would not be faith.

So I went to church each Sunday hoping for a miracle. That same day, a Prophetic lady spoke to me and stated because of my faithfulness, God is going to bless me with a big house and a good paying job. I lost faith right at that moment. I stated that "The prophecy has gone too far". It just seem impossible to me because I was struggling and having a hard time paying a 475.00 rent and no one seemed to want to give me a job. Now how could I believe that God would give me a big house? I just left the thought alone. Shortly on the day before the marshals were suppose to put me out, I begin to put my faith to work and praise God in advance for showing up with the 2 months rent I needed (calling those things which be not as though they were) because I was determined to stand on God's Word because that was my only hope.

Just as sure as the Word was spoken, the next day a lady came to my house and said God wanted her to give me something. It was the 2 month's rent I had believed God for, Wow! I rejoiced and I had received my miracle. But to my surprise that was not all God had for me because he had promised me a big house and a good paying job, but my faith wasn't there yet. So I took the money the lady brought to my house, and I went to give the money to the leasing manager to pay the past 2 months rent, but to my surprise the leasing manager refused it. He stated that I did not have a job, and He did not want to go through the eviction process with me again, and he wanted to just retain the unit. I was devastated at his response. The greatest day had become my worst day. Yet God was creating another opportunity for me to receive His promised, and it was now going to take faith. Me walking out the spoken word.

I thought all day long about the prophetic word the lady spoke to me about God giving me a house and a good paying job. I had just received the miracle I had been believing God for (the two months' rent) and I knew if I would just believe, I could possibly get the house that was promised me. I knew I had to move because the leasing manager did not take my 2 months' rent payment, and he wanted the unit back.

That night I begin to pray and I knew without a doubt it was time to walk out on the word and get the miracle God had with my name on it. I woke up the next day, and I made up my mind that I am going to live for God, and whatever he says I am going to do it. I went out that day calling up houses for rent, and realtors, and believing God for this miracle. I knew by 3:00pm that Thursday afternoon, I was going to have to find this house because tomorrow I would be put out and my kids and I would not have a place to live.

So I begin driving around looking for a house, and networking. I stumbled across a number where a lady knew someone who had a house for rent, and I spoke with the lady. She stated to me that she had a house for rent that was 3 bedrooms, and for some reason she could rent out all her other houses, but this particular one she could never rent. So she rented me the 3 bedrooms for 600.00. This house was huge. It had a huge pouch, a huge bedroom with a Jacuzzi, and a large deck in the back of the house. I move in the next day, and the next month I received that good paying job where they allowed me to get in their telecommute program, and work from home.

This was an amazing experience, and I am so glad that I took God at his word because I know for sure he will never lie, and he will never fail us when we put our trust in him. We serve and awesome God. Whatever he has been telling you, DO IT. Receive your blessing, and miracle with your name on it!

Chapter Ten

Salvation is Now

You don't have to wait until the trumpet blows, and Jesus Christ comes out of the cloud before you can receive him. The time is NOW when you decide here on earth where you will live eternally. Your choice is either Heaven or Hell, or Life or Death. Jesus helps you decide. He said, "Choose Life."

In order to go to heaven, you have to receive Jesus Christ. *(John 3:16).*

Salvation is a gift from God. Salvation is available for everyone and not just for someone who sinned a little bit or such as told a white lie. Nor is salvation for someone who might have committed a series of horrible crimes, who you might say sinned a lot.

'Ail have Sinned and falling short of God's Glory (Romans 3:23)

God loved mankind so much that He sent Jesus to save us from our sins, and he promised that we could have eternal life.

'For God so loved the world that he gave his only begotten son, that whosoever believeth in him should not perish, but have everlasting lift." John 3:16)

As long as we live in sin, we live below the standard that God had purpose for us to live. We live in darkness which is a life control by the sinful nature. As long as we choose a life of sin to be our master, we will never come into the light, and receive the abundant life that Jesus came that we may receive. *'The thief cometh not, butler to steal, to kill, and destroy. I am come that they might have life, and that they might have it more abundantly." (John 10:10)*

So Jesus states a question? What profits a person to gain the whole world and lose their soul? So many people are on the broad and spacious road that leads to destruction because we don't understand God's Plan for our life.

'For I know the thoughts that I think to2vardyou, saith the Lord, thoughts of peace, and not of evil, to give you an expected end."
(Jeremiah 29:11)

We are trying to find happiness and success in relationships. Some are trying to receive the American dream by working several jobs, while others are staying in school, and others are just robbing Peter to pay Paul waiting on their big break from the lotto. The point is, what can the world offer you in exchange for your soul. God has promised, if you would receive his Son Jesus that you will have an abundant life. The reason God is able to make this promise is because *'The Earth is the Lord and the fullness thereof the world, and they that dwells therein." (Psalms 24:1)*
He owns it all and created it all for you so that you would enjoy life to the fullest.

Thou wilt show me the path of life: in presence is fullness of joy; at thy right hand there are pleasures for evermore. (Psalms 16:11,).

The enemy called Satan uses all types of methods to enticed and distract you by tempting you with things that will bring self fulfillment, riches, and he has a way of opening doors that lead to sinful pleasures so that you will think you are enjoying life.

'Love not the world, neither the things that are in the world If any man love the world, the love of the father is not in him. For all that if in the world, the lust of the flesh, and the lust of the yes, and the pride of life. (1 John 2: 15-16).

This influence is design to keep you from searching after the true and living God. If we truly realize the price Jesus paid so that we could have our sins forgiving and not go to hell., we would get back in a right relationship with God by receiving Jesus, and possess everything heaven has to offer us.

Adam and Eve lived in the Garden and the bible states they did not want are need for anything because God was their source, and He supplied every need. *(Genesis 2:9)*

Salvation is basically Jesus paying mankind sin debt. After Adam and Eve listen to the devil lies and was influence to eat the fruit from the tree, and disobeyed God; who promised that the day you eat from the forbidden tree, you shall surely die. Adam and Eve were kicked out the garden of Eden. *(Genesis 3:23-24).*

Mankind had a sin penalty that needed to be paid. Jesus made that payment with his life.

'Therefore doth my Father love me, because I lay down my life, that I might take it again. No man taketh it from me, but I lay it down of myself I have power to lay it down, and I have power to take it again. This commandment have I received of my Father. (John 10: 17-18). He is the mediator that brings mankind back in relationship with God.

"For there is one God, and one mediator between God and men, the man Christ Jesus:" (1 Timothy 2:5)

God wishes that everyone be saved and not perish because there are two fathers: Father God and Father Devil. Father God wants your soul to be saved so you will not perish and spend eternity in Hell with the devil, but that you will spend eternity in Heaven. *(John 3:16).* Father Devil, on the other hand, does not want you to receive eternal life and he is using persuasive words and situations to turn you to serving him so you can spend eternity in hell with him and his angels in the burning fire.

"And the devil that deceived them was cast into the lake of fire and brimstone, where the beast and the false prophet are, and shall be tormented day and night forever and ever. (Revelation 20:10)

Hell is real and the Devil tries to cover it up so that you will not see how painful it would be to be left there for eternity. *'Be sober, be vigilant,. because your adversary the devil, as a roaring lion, walketh about, seeking whom he may devour" (1 Peter 5:8)*

Hell was not made for mankind, but for the Devil and His falling angels (demons) that rebelled against God in heaven, and was kicked out of heaven.
So if you disobey God and have not repented of your sins and receive Jesus into your heart, you will not have eternal life, but will suffer in the burning lake of fire.

"And whosoever was not found written in the book of 10 was cast into the lake of fire. (Revelation 20:15).

It's your choice. God is not going to choose for you. You make your choice down here on earth.

God is so loving and excited about you receiving his son Jesus that he helps you make the right decision about salvation. *"And if it seems evil unto you to serve the Lord, choose you this day whom ye will serve. Joshua 24:15)*
Jesus gives you the answer and He said choose life.

"Jesus is the truth, the life, and the way. (John 14:6)

Jesus lets you know He is the Truth, and every knee will bow before him and because He is the Truth that means every other spirit is a Lie. Jesus is the one God sent to be the savior and redeemer of all mankind.

"And thou shalt know that I the Lord am thy Savior and thy Redeemer" (Isaiah 60:16)

God gave Jesus power and authority, and Jesus is sitting at the right hand of God interceding on your behalf.

Also, if this is not convincing enough, Heaven had already come in agreement that Jesus would save God's people. *"And this is the record that God bath given to us eternal /0, and this life is in his Son. He that bath the Son bath life, and he that bath not the Son bath not life. (1 John 5:11)*

There is no other name that one can be saved, but by Jesus.

'Neither is there salvation in one other: for there is none other name under heaven given among men, 2vhereby we must be saved" (Acts 4:12)

Jesus promised that in His father's house that there are many mansions and He is preparing a place for you to go when you leave this earth. *('John 14:2).*

You will never make it into your heavenly home without receiving Jesus Christ.

The next question you may be asking is what must I do to be saved? "Then Peter said unto them, repent and be baptized every one of you in the name of Jesus Christ for the remission of sins, and ye shall receive the gift of the Holy Ghost. *(Act 2:38)*

This is your day of salvation. Today if ye will hear his voice, harden not your heart. (Psalms *95:7)*

Invite Jesus Christ into your heart today. Repent of all your sins, and make him Lord over your life. He will save you and give you a new life. "therefore if any man be in Christ he is a new creature: old things are passed away; behold, all things are become new: " *(2 Corinthians 5:17)*

Let Jesus give you a makeover today. The Kingdom of God is Righteousness, Peace, and Joy in the Holy Ghost. *(Romans 14:17)*

Will you give your life to Jesus and become born again in the spirit of Peace, Love, Joy, and unity?

When you receive Jesus, He will give you:

- Power to be called a son of God
- He will give you a new life
- His blessing will make you rich and add no sorrows
- He will give you peace that passes all understanding
- He will pick you up when you fall
- He will heal and restore you from all your past hurts
- Most of all, He will never leave you nor forsake you

Let The Redeemed Of The Lord Say, So!

Songs of Deliverance

"0 sing unto the LORD a new song; for he hath done marvelous things; his right hand, and his holy arm, hath gotten him the victory."
Psalms 98:1

FORGET NOT ALL HIS BENEFITS:
(Psalms 103:2)

The Morning Dew

Song One

The Morning Dew
(Hosea 6:1, Genesis 27:28)

This is a prophetic Word that was given to me from the Lord when trouble seemed to surround me on every side. This Word was God's way of introducing me into my morning season.

> *'Weeping may endure for a night,*
> *but joy cometh in the morning."*
> *(Psalm 30:5)*

This is the day that the Lord has made; come, let us rejoice and be glad in it. Again I say rejoice, for the earth is the Lord's and the fullness thereof and all that dwells in it. For God, He is the creator and sustainer of all things. So let the redeemed of the Lord say so. You must cry out loud and spare not.

Because a new day is dawning and I hear the music in the air. Your troubles, yes they are behind you, and the sky is fair. But look, the baby's coming and it's called a fresh anointing. It's the anointing that sets the captive free, that restores, that releases you into the blessings of God, where you're no longer fearing the devil, but you're only saying yes to God.

So hear the rain as it comes down and let it wash off the old you and let it cleanse you from all your past sins and all your frowns. You can now live because He lives, and I'm talking about Jesus our Lord and Jesus our Savior. So take the oil of gladness and put on the whole armor of God.

Because a new life is being formed and you've been touched by the Master, and you're destined to be His masterpiece. So let the Master renew your mind and let the Master renew your heart. And the Master, He wants to strengthen those of you who are faint and He wants to build those of you who are torn down. But you have to cast your cares upon Him for He cares so much for you.

Now begin to feel His presence as He surrounds you with His love. His love endures forever and His mercies, yes. They are everlasting and His mercies are new every day. Because God, I say God delights in you. And you, beloved, you are the apple of God's eyes and you are so precious in His sight.

So arise, and shine, for your light has come. What God needed to do, He has already done. And He knows the plans that He has for you and they are marvelous in His sight. You are no longer a victim, but you are victorious, you are a child of light. You are more than a conqueror because greater is He that's in you and you can do all things through Jesus Christ, the God that will strengthen you.

Now take His peace as He gives it to you. You are no longer bound and the tears that you have, yes, they are tears of joy. Receive all that God has for you. You are a born again eagle, begin to fly high. There is nothing that can stop you. The devil has tried and he's missed over and over. You were born to succeed.

So walk in your purpose and into your destiny, and begin to help those who are coming behind you and you be free. It's no longer you, but it's He, Jesus the Christ that died for you and Jesus that died for me and shed His blood on Calvary. Oh, great is Thy faithfulness towards us men!

For we know that the kingdom of God suffereth violence, but the violent take it back by force. We overcome by the blood of the Lamb and the word of all our testimonies.

Go on and testify. Every soldier has a war story of how He brought us over and how He's kept us, for He's a keeper, I say, the keeper of your soul.

Go on and shout the victory, and know that your labor is not in vain because it's only what you do for Jesus Christ that will last. And He's given you power over every form of evil, power over the enemy. He's equipped you with all spiritual blessings. You are a joint-heir with Jesus Christ. So take authority, for if God be for you who can be against you.

Oh praise the Lord, I say praise the Lord, oh my soul, and all that's within me. And bless His holy name for He is so worthy of all the praise. Not for what He has done, but just simply for Who God is: He's Jehovah Jireh — your provider, Jehovah Shalom — your peace, El Shaddai — your all sufficient God, Jehovah Rapha, - your healer, El Elyon — The God that sets you up on high, Jehovah Nissi — your banner, and most of all:

The Lord, He is your Shepherd and in Him you shall not want, He'll make you to lie down in green pastures, He restores your soul, He leads you by the still waters, He leads you in the path of righteousness for His name's sake. Though you walk through the valley of the shadow of death, you should fear no evil, for He is with you. His rod and staff shall comfort you. God has prepared a table before you in the presence of your enemies; God has anointed your head with oil; your cup runneth over, and surely goodness and mercy will follow you all the days of your life, and you will dwell in the house of the Lord forever. Amen.

Song Two

Surrender

Your arms are too short to box with God. God has a perfect plan for our lives, and when we try to fight God and not do His will, we become burdened, full of anxiety, and our soul begins to cry out for God, Abba Father. *(Romans 8:15)*

Each time I hear You calling me, Your call is strong on my life, You see, Your voice is so deep inside me. It says, "You have to leave that what you used to be if you want to be totally free." I fall down so many times and I just keep telling you all kinds of lies. I repent about all my wrongs just so that I can stay strong. Really I'm afraid that I won't last long and that's the reason for this song.

Oh, You are beautiful and Your melodies are too. I feel Your peace in the inner part of me and Your wisdom cries, "Victory" that makes me free. I know You are the truth, the life, and the way, and You will not put more on me than I can take. You have always made a way for me to escape. So come and guide me in the upper room where only eagles can fly because it's way in the sky, high above turbulence and destruction and high above anything that's not alive. You are life and You are <u>full</u> of creativity. Continue to show off in me. There's no reason for me to wait around.

So, today, Lord, I lay all my burdens down. I'm on my knees asking You to forgive me please, and in need of your strong hand to deliver me from this flesh of mine that just doesn't want to die. And Your Word tells me to renew my mind.

(Psalms 34:15-19):

The eyes of the LORD are upon the righteous, and his ears are open unto their cry. The face of the LORD is against them that do evil, to cut off the remembrance of them from the earth. The righteous cry, and the LORD heareth, and delivereth them out of all their troubles. The LORD is nigh unto them that are of a broken heart; and saveth such as be of a contrite spirit.

Many are the afflictions of the righteous: but the LORD delivereth him out of them all.

I surrender, I surrender, I surrender

All my dreams seem to be shattered and in the back of my ear I can hear the enemies' laughter. But all I end up with is tears in my eyes because my soul cries for You each and every time. Lord, I surrender because my life has been brought with a price by the blood of Jesus Christ. Thank You Lord for loving me.

So long a time it's been, for so long I waited to begin and all I can do is remember when: You saved me when my life was a mess. You sheltered me when I was homeless. You gave me rest when I was not at my best, just so I could pass my test. You supplied every one of my needs and You gave me the victory. All You ask is that I believe in Your Son who can save a wretch like me. A wretch undone.

(Psalms 25:1-10)
Unto thee, 0 LORD, do I lift up my soul. 0 my God, I trust in thee: let me not be ashamed, let not mine enemies triumph over me. Yea, let none that wait on thee be ashamed: let them be ashamed which transgress without cause. Show me thy ways, 0 LORD; teach me thy paths. Lead me in thy truth, and teach me: for thou art the God of my salvation; on thee do I wait all the day.

Remember, 0 LORD, thy tender mercies and thy loving-kindnesses; for they have been ever of old. Remember not the sins of my youth, nor my transgressions: according to thy mercy remember thou me for thy goodness' sake, 0 LORD. Good and upright is the LORD: therefore will he teach sinners in the way. The meek will he guide in judgment: and the meek will he teach his way.

All the paths of the LORD are mercy and truth unto such as keep his covenant and his testimonies.

I know this much is true: there is no other God like You, who could love me the way You do. You are so faithful and just, and I need you so much.

I surrender (high soprano)

Thank You for being there, and that's the reason for this prayer:

Father, I come in the name of Jesus asking You to forgive me of all my sins. Forgive me of every wrong thought, every wrong intention of my heart, and purge me, oh Lord. You said In your Word that if I believe in my heart and confess with my mouth that You are Jesus Christ, then I will be saved. Create in me a clean heart and renew a right spirit within me. Wash me in Your precious blood and cleanse me from all unrighteousness. Thank You Lord for saving me, and for all Your grace and all Your mercy. Thank You for a second chance to experience Your redemption power, peace and liberty. Today, my will I surrender.

THE END

If my people, which are called by my name, shall humble themselves, and pray, and seek Ng face, and turn from their wicked ways, then will I hear from heaven, and will forgive their sin, and will heal their land." (2 Chronicles 7:14)

About The Author

Michelle Murray was born and raised in the Harlem area of New York City. She graduated from LaGuardia Community College in 1986. She received her writing diploma from The Institute of Children's Literature in 1988. In 1998, Michelle surrendered her life to Jesus, and has lived in Atlanta, Georgia since 1994. She attends The True Light Baptist Church, "where miracles really do happen." She is a facilitator in the New Member's Ministry.

Michelle was selected from her Church to receive the "2005, Women Who Beat The Odds Award", from the Concern Black Clergy.

CPSIA information can be obtained
at www.ICGtesting.com
Printed in the USA
FFOW02n2042270415
12984FF